Winston Churchill

A Biography of one of history's most iconic men

Matt Clarke

Table of Contents

Introduction 1

Chapter 1: Child 3

Chapter 2: Student 8

Chapter 3: Soldier 14

Chapter 4: Hero 21

Chapter 5: Politician 31

Chapter 6: World War I 39

Chapter 7: Private Life 57

Chapter 8: World War II 59

Chapter 9: Post WWII 69

Chapter 10: Legacy 73

Conclusion 79

Introduction

Sir Winston Leonard Spencer Churchill was born on November 30, 1874 and passed away on January 24, 1965. He lived a variegated and full life and is marked as one of the most remarkable men in history.

During his time in Parliament, he represented a total of five different constituencies. He was a member of both the Conservative and Liberal Parties during his political career. He also served in several positions, namely President of the Board of Trade, Home Secretary, Chancellor of the Duchy of Lancaster, First Lord of the Admiralty, Minister of Munitions, Secretary of State for War, Secretary of State for Air, Secretary of State for the Colonies, Chancellor of the Exchequer, and Prime Minister. Outside of politics, Churchill also served in the military.

During his time in office, Winston Churchill was responsible for many shifts in British law. He was responsible for the Coal Mines Regulation Act 1908. This act established an 8-hour day in all mines. Churchill also established the first minimum wage system in Britain with the Trade Boards Act 1909. He was responsible for the Labour Exchanges Act 1909, which set up offices to help unemployed people find work. Churchill also instituted the

National Insurance Act 1911, providing sickness and unemployment benefits.

Winston Churchill was a figure deeply involved in both World War I and World War II. His roles in both are considered by many to be crucial in the victories against the Germans.

Winston Churchill loved to write. He began his writing career as a journalistic war correspondent. Later, he wrote several books on a variety of topics, including history, his father's biography, his own exploits, the war, political difficulties, and a generally unknown work of fiction. In addition, Winston Churchill indulged in painting. He would often submit his artwork under a pseudonym so the art would be evaluated on its own merits.

Winston Churchill was a colorful and vigorous character who lived his life to the fullest and left his mark on history.

Chapter 1: Child

Winston Churchill was born on the evening of the 30th of November, 1874. He was born at Blenheim Palace, delivered in a cloakroom after his mother was rushed from the ballroom, having gone into premature labor.

His father, Lord Randolph Churchill, was twenty-five years old. He had married Jeanette Jerome, a beautiful American girl, seven months prior, in April of that year.

To better understand the influences that shaped Winston Leonard Spencer Churchill, it is necessary to touch upon his family heritage.

John Churchill

Winston Churchill's ancestors arrived in England with William the Conqueror in the eleventh century. John Churchill, the first Duke of Marlborough, was the founder of the family's fame in the seventeenth century. John Churchill led English armies to many victories. He was known for his courage and diplomatic skill, which earned him both military and political advancement.

Winston Churchill was no doubt influenced by his ancestor's achievements. The fact that he held a great interest in John Churchill's life is evident by the fact that Winston Churchill wrote his biography, *Marlborough: His Life and Times*. The biography initially comprised four well-researched volumes first published in 1933.

John Churchill's career spanned across the reign of several monarchs. He faced many challenges, both in political and military terms. He was acclaimed in times of war, but during times of peace, he was often the target of plots.

Randolph Churchill

Winston Churchill's father was the other primary influence on his life. Though they never developed a close personal relationship, Winston was keenly aware of all that transpired in his father's life. Winston published his father's biography, titled *Lord Randolph Churchill*, in 1906.

Lord Randolph Churchill's initial political career was unremarkable. A year after Winston's birth, a clash with the Prince of Wales, who would become King Edward VII, changed Randolph. Lord Blandford, Randolph's brother, had become the lover of the Prince of Wales' former mistress. The Prince was angered and tried to get the woman's husband to sue for divorce, naming Lord Blandford in the scandal. Lord Randolph came to his brother's defense, stating that a divorce case would bring to light letters written by the Prince himself.

The Prince of Wales did not take kindly to the threat and stated he would not enter the home of anyone who entertained either of the Churchill brothers. It was a statement that effectively exiled them from aristocratic circles.

The Duke of Marlborough, Randolph's father, accepted the position of Viceroy in Ireland and took Randolph with him as his private secretary. And so, young Winston spent the first few years of his life in Dublin. Upon their return, Lord Randolph once again took up his place in Parliament. Where once he was disinterested, he now used his position as a platform to attack his aristocratic tormentors. He spoke out against his party as well as the Opposition Party, rising rapidly to national prominence. With his political stock rising, Lord Randolph and his family settled in London. Here, in their small rented house, young Winston Churchill met many political figures.

Lord Randolph's political tactics were unorthodox. He refused to hold his tongue, a habit that his son would mimic. Lord Randolph was physically unimpressive. He made up for this through sheer force of personality and oratory skills, both of which young Winston observed closely.

Randolph's Resignation

Lord Randolph's stormy career reached its peak when he was appointed as Chancellor of the Exchequer. In this position, it was his responsibility to prepare the governmental budget. In his usual fashion, Lord Randolph attempted violent reforms. He attacked the military budget, demanding cuts in expenditure. The War Ministry refused his proposed cuts. Lord Randolph announced that he would resign if the cuts to the Army's budget were not permitted. He was confident in his position, and threatening resignation was a tactic he had used before to get his way.

Unfortunately for Lord Randolph, his bluff was called, and his resignation was accepted. He remained in Parliament, though his political career was destroyed by his own doing. Lord Randolph, who had been viewed as the next Prime Minister, faded into obscurity. It was a fall that greatly influenced Winston Churchill's political career.

Early Childhood

Winston Churchill spent the first few years of his life in Dublin, raised by a nurse. His father busied himself with politics while his mother spent her time as a fashionable socialite. They did, however, give Winston many toys, his favorite of which was a set of a thousand tin soldiers.

Even when Lord Randolph returned to London after his ostracism, Winston saw very little of his father. He grew up a chubby, solemn-looking child. In Winston's sixth year, his younger brother John was born. John Churchill never entered public life. He became a stockbroker.

Chapter 2: Student

Winston Churchill's parents, like all parents, had high hopes for their son's education. Being of aristocratic birth, this was even more true in Winston's case. His parents had hoped that Winston would eventually enter the prestigious school of Eton. However, Winston Churchill's path through the education system was unexpected, mostly due to Winston himself.

St. James's School

At the age of seven, Winston Churchill was sent to St. James's School. An expensive, modern, well-equipped boarding school in Ascot, St. James's was a preparatory school for Eton.

As it turned out, Winston hated everything about this school. He hated the schoolmasters, the discipline, and the studies. The school believed in flogging. Yet receiving several canings did little to quell Winston's rebellious and independent nature. Winston Churchill would often question his teachers and lead the students in mischief.

It was at St. James's where Winston had his first contact with the Latin language. After butting heads with the Latin teacher, which led to a running war, Winston grew to despise the subject, a bias that stayed with him all his life.

Churchill spent two years at St. James's. He was miserable, and the frequent canings took a toll on his health. Winston also did not seem to be making much academic progress. At the suggestion of his doctor, his parents removed him from the school.

Brighton

At the age of nine, Churchill was enrolled in a school in Brighton. The school was less discipline-oriented, something which Winston appreciated. It did not, however, quell his rebellious nature. His teachers often said he was the naughtiest boy in class. At Brighton, Winston turned out a short-lived school paper called The Critic. He also participated in amateur theater.

During his time at Brighton, Winston was permitted to visit Blenheim Palace. Blenheim Palace was now the home of his uncle, the eighth Duke of Marlborough, Lord Randolph's older brother. It was during these visits that Winston Churchill became enamored with his ancestor, John Churchill. He would reenact the first Duke of Marlborough's most famous military battles with toy soldiers. Winston was determined that his own life should be as exciting as that of John Churchill's. He wanted his name to go down in history, the same way his ancestors had.

Lord Randolph had by this time begun his political rise. Winston Churchill gained a reputation of his own, as the son of someone famous. Winston kept a scrapbook of his father's speeches. He followed his father's career closely and became his father's most staunch supporter. However, his father remained disinterested in his son. Lord Randolph saw Winston only as a troublemaker with no academic ability. He spent as little time with his son as possible.

Harrow

At age 13, Winston Churchill was sent to Harrow, not Eton. Winston had contracted pneumonia twice, and it was thought that the climate at Harrow would be better suited to someone with weak lungs. Winston was admitted into the school but not by his academic merits. It was his father's reputation that granted him entrance.

Winston was at the bottom of his class academically, a place he remained in for the five years he spent at Harrow. Winston remained opinionated and arrogant. He would argue openly with his teachers. Winston still despised the Latin language and avoided Greek as well. Although Winston swam and rode horses well, he avoided team sports.

Winston did, however, discover a love of the English language. It began with the novels of H. Rider Haggard. From there, he began reading the English classics. Later on, in one of the books he authored, Winston Churchill would thank his English teacher, Mr. Somervell. He appears to have spent most of his spare time reading.

With Winston's dismal academic record, his father was concerned about Winston's future. When his son was home on vacation, playing with his toy soldiers and plotting out complex battles, Lord Randolph approached him with a question. He asked whether Winston would like to become a soldier himself. Winston was ecstatic, believing his father saw in him the potential of a military genius. In truth, Lord Randolph saw a military career as the only suitable option for his son, whom he believed might be mentally hampered.

Winston spent his last three years at Harrow in Army Class, in preparation for the Royal Military Academy, Sandhurst. Unfortunately, Winston failed the entrance exam for Sandhurst twice. Frustrated, Lord Randolph sent Winston to a crammer, who gave him intensive coaching. Finally, on his third attempt, Winston was accepted.

Sandhurst

His father had hoped Winston would join the 60th Rifles. However, Winston's grades were so low that he was only able to join the cavalry. The cavalry's regiment standards were lower than any other regiments. While his father may have been disappointed, Winston, on the other hand, was delighted. He enjoyed horse riding and would now be entitled to a horse of his own.

For the first time, Winston responded to an academic environment. With traditional subjects removed from his curriculum, Winston's studies focused on subjects he found more appealing. He learned of military law, topography, reading military maps, tactics, and fortifications. There were also many drills on horseback.

The Royal Military Academy, Sandhurst, was an aristocratic school. Winston's classmates included people such as the future King Alfonso XIII of Spain, and the Crown Prince of Siam. As the son of a Lord and with his notable ancestry, Winston Churchill would not have felt out of place. However, maintaining Winston at Sandhurst was a great financial strain. Winston was aware of this and attempted to make the most of his education there. He displayed none of his previous rebellious behavior and endeavored to work hard on his studies. While on vacation, he took additional equestrian training with the Royal Horse Guards at Knightsbridge Barracks, in London. Winston even ranked fourth amongst the cavalry candidates. In the end, Winston graduated eighth in a class of 150. Sadly, Lord Randolph passed away two months before Winston Churchill received his first commission. Winston grieved bitterly at the loss of his father, who died at the young age of 45.

Chapter 3: Soldier

Winston Churchill was now 20 years old. He was commissioned into the 4th Queen's Own Hussars. It was a regiment composed of aristocrats. An officer's year consisted of seven months of training and five months of winter leave. Officers spent their time floating through the fashionable social circles of the upper class during their winter leave.

Unfortunately, Lord Randolph did not leave much of an estate. Even so, Winston's mother gave him an allowance each year. He also earned a small wage as an officer. This income, however, was not enough to sustain the cost of his expected social life. Winston began to grow restless.

Cuba

At this point, the only military action happening in the world was taking place in Cuba. The Cuban people had risen in revolt against Spain, who was in control of the land. It was a small-scale war, with only a few thousand soldiers on each side. Nevertheless, Winston was eager to see action. His mother helped him get in touch with Sir Henry Drummond-Wolff, the

British Ambassador to Spain.

Winston Churchill convinced the Ambassador to get him introduced to the Spanish authorities in Havana. Churchill then contacted the *Daily Graphic*, a newspaper, offering his services as a correspondent. Churchill also convinced Reginald Barnes, a 4th Hussars comrade, to accompany him. Winston Churchill and Reginald Barnes set sail for Cuba on November 3, 1895.

After spending two days at a hotel in Havana, sampling the cigars, they finally decided to introduce themselves to the Spanish authorities. The Spaniards spoke limited English, and Churchill and his companion spoke no Spanish at all. The Spaniards, through a misunderstanding, welcomed them as emissaries, and Churchill did little to correct them. It was arranged that they would journey inland to meet up with a Spanish force of 4000 men, led by General Valdez. Churchill and Barnes met up with the Spanish forces and set out in pursuit of Cuban rebels.

The Spanish army came under sporadic fire for several days, something which Churchill found himself enjoying. He sent several dispatches back to the *Daily Graphic*, detailing his experiences. Naturally, these dispatches were heavily peppered with his opinions.

General Valdez and the Spanish army pursued the rebels, who eventually disappeared into the jungle, marking the end of the campaign. Before their departure home, the Spaniards presented Churchill and Barnes with the Order of Military Merit, First Class.

Northwest Frontier

The 4th Queen's Own Hussars were shipped to India several months later. The daily routine there left Churchill with a lot of spare time, most of which he spent reading. Once again, Churchill grew restless. He obtained leave for three months and returned to England, hoping to secure a more exciting assignment.

While in London, conflict broke out in the Northwest Frontier of India. The Pashtun tribesmen had declared jihad on the British and began attacking their camps around the Malakand Pass. The Malakand Pass was a strategic point, the loss of which would threaten British control of the area.

Churchill contacted Sir Bindon, the man in charge of dealing with the rebellion. While Sir Bindon had no active military posts available for Churchill to serve in, he invited Churchill to join as a war correspondent. Churchill returned to Bombay and convinced a local paper, the *Allahabad Pioneer*, to hire him. His mother in London secured him a position as a war correspondent from the *Daily Telegraph*. Churchill then secured an extension on his leave and set out to join Sir Bindon on the Northwest Frontier.

Churchill joined the unit known as the Malakand Field Force. On the first day of the march, they were attacked by tribesmen. Winston sprang into action, wielding a sword and pistol. The fighting continued for several hours, leaving the Malakand Field Force almost out of ammunition and surrounded. When it seemed like they would be overwhelmed, the 11th Bengal Lancers rode onto the scene and routed the tribesmen.

Churchill continued to fight alongside the Malakand Field Force for several weeks. During this time, he sent to the two newspapers dispatches that became widely acclaimed. Eventually, the rebellion was quelled, and the Malakand Field Force disbanded. Winston Churchill returned to Bangalore, India. There he began work on his first major literary endeavor, *The Story of the Malakand Field Force*. In this book, he detailed his time in the field. True to form, Churchill was unafraid to criticize the British Army. It was a bold move, considering he was only a junior officer. The book was widely read and received praise. However, Churchill's superior officers were naturally none too pleased.

Sudan

During those years, Sudan was ruled by an English army of occupation. A Mahdist movement and its dervish armies rose in rebellion. They had succeeded in decimating the Egyptian army commanded by the English commander, General C. G. Gordon. In the spring of 1898, plans had begun to liberate Sudan. The Commander-in-Chief of the Anglo-Egyptian Army, Sir Herbert Kitchener, planned on leading six brigades into Sudan to take the area back.

Churchill was once again eager to join in active combat. However, Sir Kitchener refused to have him. Sir Kitchener read *The Story of the Malakand Field Force* and wanted nothing to do with the young upstart who publicly criticized his superiors. Not even a letter from Churchill's mother could convince Sir Kitchener.

Churchill did not give up. He contacted Sir Evelyn Wood, the Adjutant-General. By way of a loophole in army rank, Sir Wood secured a place for Churchill. Churchill was assigned to the 21st Lancers as a lieutenant and ordered to report to Cairo. Not one to miss an opportunity, Churchill approached the *Morning Post* for an assignment to report on the campaign before setting off to Cairo.

Winston Churchill arrived in Cairo and was put in charge of the mess store. The troops set out on the journey to Omdurman. When they got close, they got their first view of the enemy. Amassing on the plain outside the city were 60,000 dervishes. Churchill was ordered to ride back seven miles to bring the news to Sir Kitchener. Churchill was nervous, not knowing how Sir Kitchener would react to the fact that he had come to Sudan after all. He delivered his report, was asked a few questions, and then dismissed. As it turned out, Sir Kitchener did not know who the young lieutenant was.

The battle began at dawn. Although the British were outnumbered three to one, they had the distinct advantage of modern artillery and guns. Their opponents had only lances and swords. Within the first hour, 20,000 dervishes lay dead and wounded.

Churchill had done little in that first hour but watch. That changed with the order for the 21st Lancers to go forward and mop up any survivors. Churchill rode out with 300 men, straight into an ambush. Out of hiding, 2,000 dervishes rose and attacked. With sabers drawn, the 21st Lancers committed themselves to the charge. It was a fierce clash in which 75 men and more than a hundred horses were lost. However, the dervishes suffered severe casualties. The fight lasted only a few minutes before the dervishes broke and fled to the city.

Retirement from the Army

Winston decided the time had arrived for him to begin his political career. He was satisfied that he had seen and fought in a sufficient number of campaigns. He resolved to leave the army and enter public life. As far as he was concerned, there was nothing more for him to gain from remaining in a military position. He would not be given any important promotions due to his outspoken nature. Churchill decided his next battles would take place in the House of Commons.

Upon his return to India, Churchill resigned from his regiment. He then wrote a book titled *The River War* covering the Sudan campaign. In the book, as before, Churchill thrashed his superiors, including Sir Kitchener. Despite Sir Kitchener's rage, the book did well. It received much praise outside of military circles. Churchill returned and settled in London, now a civilian and an established writer.

Chapter 4: Hero

Some understanding of the British Parliamentary system is required to understand Winston Churchill's role in the political arena. Parliament in Britain is divided into two Houses, the House of the Lords, which is hereditary, and the House of Commons, which is elective.

In ages past, the House of Lords held significant power in governance. A power shift took place during Churchill's political career. The House of Commons took power with the House of Lords and the Monarchy shifting to a purely advisory and ceremonial role. There is also another difference between American and British legislative systems. In America, members of Congress must reside in the state that they represent. In Britain, members of Parliament do not have to live in the districts that they run to represent.

The Monarch invites the leader of the party with the largest representation in Parliament to serve as Prime Minister and create a government. In America, the independently elected President appoints a non-elected Cabinet. But in Britain, the Prime Minister and his Cabinet must all be members of Parliament. When the Prime Minister no longer has the majority support in the House of Commons, he must resign and allow a new Prime Minister to form a government. No government is allowed to sit for more than five years.

Taste of Politics

Winston Churchill had made his mind up to enter Parliament. He let the leaders of the Conservative Party know that he was available for service. Winston was invited to run in the place of a member who had fallen ill. He had little experience in campaigning. The topic he had chosen for his speeches did not impress the voters of Oldham. Oldham itself was a Liberal district, composed mostly of working-class people. The campaign was a disastrous one, and the Conservative Party lost both seats.

It was not a very good beginning to Winston Churchill's political career. Churchill had not made a good impression on the established powers. He also became the center of a controversy in Conservative circles after he refused to align with their policies on the Tithes Bill.

With this initial failure in hand, Churchill returned to his journalistic pursuits. It would not be too long, however, before another war was on the horizon.

Anglo-Boer War

South Africa had two republics founded by the Boers, Dutch farmers who had settled the area in the 17th century. These were the Orange Free State and the Transvaal. British settlers who arrived later had established colonies of their own around the Cape of Good Hope. Gradually the British had begun drifting into Boer territory as a result of the gold discovered there.

Friction arose because the Boers were determined to remain independent. Joseph Chamberlain, the Colonial Secretary, wanted to unite the different republics into one federation under British rule. Chamberlain was in discussions with Paul Kruger, the leader of the Boers. Chamberlain wanted British subjects living in the Transvaal to be granted citizenship after five years. Kruger initially agreed but attached conditions to his acceptance—conditions which Joseph Chamberlain could not accept. It seemed as though war would be inevitable.

Joseph Chamberlain sent 10,000 troops to South Africa to reinforce the British soldiers already stationed there. Paul Kruger insisted that he withdraw the troops, laying down an ultimatum. The deadline for the ultimatum passed on October 12, 1899, and war was officially declared. The big prize was the rich gold and diamond fields around Johannesburg.

When news of Kruger's ultimatum broke, Winston Churchill wasted no time. He had been asked by the *Morning Post* to travel to South Africa and act as their correspondent, with an offer for very generous compensation. The Liberal Party had declared the war shameful oppression of free people. The Conservative Party was split on the war. Churchill, on the other hand, remained neutral about the war. He was less concerned about the justice of the venture and more concerned about being where the action was.

Churchill expected the war to be a short one. How could farmers stand up to trained, well-armed British soldiers? He expressed his concern to a new friend, John Atkins, as they sailed to Cape Town. Atkins was a reporter for the *Guardian*. The Boers surprised everyone, however, fighting with unexpected skill. They invaded the British colony of Natal and laid siege to the town of Ladysmith.

Chieveley Ambush

Winston Churchill and John Atkins set out to Ladysmith shortly after making landfall in South Africa. They arrived in a nearby town, Escourt, held by the British. The British commander at Escourt had decided on a bizarre course of action. He wanted to send out cavalry to scout north towards Ladysmith. An armored train moving along a railway of 16 miles (26 kilometers) would be dispatched to back the cavalry. The slow-moving train was armed only with rifles and one six-pound naval gun. It was an easy target that could be stranded far from its base by simply blowing up a stretch of railway track.

Captain Haldane, who was in charge of this expedition, invited both Churchill and Atkins to accompany him. Atkins politely refused, saying that they were sure to be captured. Churchill agreed that the expedition was foolish but agreed to go all the same.

The first 14 miles (19 kilometers) of the expedition went well. But at the station of Chieveley, the Boers launched an ambush. They opened fire on the train with a pom-pom gun, two small artillery guns, and 300 rifles. As the train rolled forward on the tracks, it ran into a shell. The explosion derailed several cars and the engine was pinned in the wreckage.

As the British returned fire, Churchill worked with a volunteer crew to free the train. They worked for an hour under enemy fire to free the engine. Loading the wounded onto the train, they began making their way back towards Escourt. The soldiers who were not wounded walked behind the train on the tracks.

Churchill, though not wounded, was aboard the train. The train began to outpace the marching soldiers until there was a gap of around a quarter of a mile. Seeing this, Churchill ordered the engineer to stop the train. He hopped off to go and check on Captain Haldane and his exhausted soldiers.

The Boers suddenly launched a second attack, sweeping down from the surrounding hills. Churchill immediately ducked into a ravine, crawling along as fast as he was able. A Boer on horseback appeared and leveled his rifle at Churchill, demanding he surrender. Churchill had left his pistol on the train and was unarmed. He had no choice but to comply.

Churchill, Captain Haldane, and several soldiers were taken prisoner that day. The Boer horseman that captured Churchill was Louis Botha. Louis Botha would later become the Prime Minister of the Union of South Africa.

Prisoner of War

When Churchill was taken prisoner, he feared for his life. As a civilian who had participated in military action, he thought the Boers might execute him on the spot. The Boers had other plans, sending him instead to Pretoria as a prisoner of war.

Churchill tried to argue his way out, claiming they had no right to imprison a civilian war correspondent. However, his actions at the train incident did not count in his favor as a non-combatant. The Boers were also aware that he was the son of a British Lord and had no intentions of releasing him. In the end, Winston talked his way into being kept a prisoner with a group of 60 British officers.

Churchill immediately began making an escape plan. He quickly realized that this would prove difficult. The guards paid close attention to him, and the State Model School where they were held was well guarded. Yet Captain Haldane and Sergeant Major Brockie had come up with a plausible escape plan. Churchill asked to be included in the escape plan. They were reluctant at first but eventually agreed. The escape plan was a simple one. They would climb through the roof of the latrine one at a time and from there leap over the wall. Once out, they would make their way across enemy territory to Portuguese East Africa. Brockie, who spoke Afrikaans and a local African language, would guide them.

Escape

The three men set aside chocolate bars, canned meat, and maps in preparation for their escape. On December 12, they put their escape plan into action. Churchill was the first to go. He managed to get over the wall and hid in some bushes as he waited for the other two men. After 30 minutes, he heard Captain Haldane whisper through the fence that they would not be able to make it, as there were too many sentries. Captain Haldane told Churchill to come back.

Churchill, however, did not see the point of climbing back into imprisonment. He decided he was going to take his chances, even though he spoke no other language besides English. With nothing but a bit of money and four chocolate bars, Churchill set out. He walked until he found railroad tracks and began following them. A freight train came along, and Churchill hopped on board. At dawn, he left the train and continued on foot. Walking the entire day under the blazing sun, he was completely exhausted. Churchill found a small mining village. He knew that Englishmen were living in some of the South African mining towns, so Churchill decided he would take a chance and knock on one of the doors. Churchill didn't see any other option since he was exhausted to the point of delirium and had no supplies.

He chose a house and knocked on the door. He began telling the man who answered some fantastic tale that he made up on the spot. The man stopped him and told him that there was no need to lie. He knew that he was Winston Churchill.

On the Run

The man whose house Churchill had approached was John Howard, an Englishman, and the only Englishman for 20 miles (32 kilometers). Had Winston chosen any other house, he would have immediately been turned in. John Howard was the manager of the Transvaal Collieries. A mine employee, Mr. Dewsnap, lived with him. Strangely enough, Mr. Dewsnap happened to be from Oldham, the same place Churchill had suffered his electoral defeat.

The Boers had not taken Churchill's escape lightly. Notices had been placed throughout Boer-controlled territory, issuing a reward for Churchill's return, dead or alive. There was an extensive manhunt to find him. News of his escape had even reached England.

John Howard hid Churchill in the mine for three days. On the fourth day, Churchill was smuggled onto a train's freight car with bales of wool. The freight was bound for Lourenco Marques, a Portuguese colony. Churchill remained in the freight car for two and a half days.

Freedom

The train crossed the border, and Churchill was delighted. He made his way to the British consul in Lourenco Marques, where he revealed his identity. They received him with jubilation, and news of his successful escape quickly spread. That evening he took a boat to Durban.

At Durban, Churchill was given a hero's welcome. There were bands on the dockside. Foghorns, whistles, and sirens sounded at his arrival. Despite all the excitement, Churchill still made time to send off telegrams. The first went to the Boer Minister of

War to report his safety. The second telegram he sent to the *Morning Post*, the newspaper whose correspondent he was. In true Churchill fashion, he added some advice to the British general staff regarding the war—advice that was naturally unwelcome given how badly the war had been going for the British to that point.

Controversial Hero

Many newspapers attacked Churchill, stating that he had put himself in danger on purpose for publicity. He was also attacked for acting as though he were still in the military, even though he was a civilian. The fact that Churchill spoke highly of the Boers, even calling them honorable, did not endear him to many people either.

Churchill brushed off these criticisms and attacks without much thought. He became an unpaid lieutenant in the South African Light Horse regiment. Churchill went on to fight in the Battle of Spion Kop and later to lift the siege on Ladysmith. The British eventually took Pretoria and Johannesburg. The Boer resistance was broken in the summer of 1900, and it seemed as though the war would soon come to an end. Churchill decided to return to England and run for a seat in the House of Commons once more.

Chapter 5: Politician

Winston Churchill was a name relatively unknown before the Anglo-Boer War. Now he was one of the most well-known men in England, and many hailed Churchill as a hero. He returned to England, preparing campaign speeches on the voyage back.

Victory in Oldham

Many constituencies had invited Churchill to make his Parliamentary run, but he chose Oldham. Churchill would be running against the same opponents as before. This time, the main election issue was the war in South Africa. Churchill kicked off his first campaign speech by recounting his escape and mentioning Mr. Dewsnap, the man from Oldham who had helped him. Churchill campaigned furiously, delivering 150 speeches in two months.

Churchill's opponents resorted to a smear campaign in an attempt to offset his popularity. Rumors that he had left the Army in disgrace and went to Africa as a correspondent because he was a coward, afraid to go as a soldier, flourished. Accusations that Churchill was a coward for leaving his companions behind in prison were also spread. Despite all this, Churchill was elected to Parliament on October 1, 1900.

Lecture Tour

Winston now faced a financial problem. Members of Parliament are unpaid. While he had made some money from the books he had published, it would not be enough to sustain him. Thus, Churchill decided to embark on a lecture tour.

He spent five weeks touring England. The subject of his lectures was the Anglo-Boer War and defending England's part in it. He was paid per lecture given. By the end of the five weeks, he had managed to bank a considerable sum of money.

Next, Churchill went to America. A promoter named Major Pond paid him a large sum of money, plus percentages. Winston shared the stage with Mark Twain. Americans were generally pro-Boer in their views, and this meant Churchill got a cold welcome. They were, however, curious to see the legendary young Englishman. Of course, the presence of Mark Twain helped as well. Overall, the tour was a great success.

The American tour ended in January 1901. Churchill had spoken every day, except Sundays, since his election in October. The lecture tours had provided him with a large-enough sum of money to sustain himself. Churchill returned to London and prepared himself to take his seat in the House of Commons.

New Era

Queen Victoria passed away on January 22, 1901. With her passing, the Victorian Era came to a close. The Prince of Wales, the very same with whom Lord Randolph had quarreled, ascended to the throne as King Edward VII. The new King formally opened Parliament a month later.

Despite the change in the Monarchy, there was little change within Parliament itself. The Conservative Party under Lord Salisbury was still firmly in control. The Liberal Party was weak and divided.

When Churchill entered the political arena, he took the position of right wing within the Conservative Party. He was a political reactionary at the start of his career. But Churchill's behavior in Parliamentary sessions was radical from the start.

The powerful figures of Parliament were much the same as they had been when Lord Randolph had been there. Lord Salisbury, the same Prime Minister who accepted Lord Randolph's resignation, was still in full control. His sons and nephew all held seats and prominent positions within the Cabinet.

Parliamentary Debut

It was customary for a new member to wait a few months before taking the floor for the first time in the House of Commons, but Winston Churchill made his debut just three days after the session had begun. It was not spectacular, but it was well-received. The debate at hand was the Anglo-Boer War. The war had turned into a guerrilla conflict and continued to drag out, draining British resources.

Churchill shrewdly fashioned his speech. He praised the Boers' courage, winning the approval of those members against the war. At the same time, he defended the Conservative Party's position. After a successful first speech, Churchill settled into Parliamentary life easily. He spoke in Parliament often in the months that followed.

At the start of his career, Winston Churchill's political positions were an exact copy of his father's. Unfortunately, those doctrines were obsolete for the time. The other influence on Churchill's political views was Sir Francis Mowatt. Sir Francis was the head of Civil Service and was a friend of Churchill's late father. Armed with their views Churchill soon found himself running counter to the official policies of the Conservative Party.

Antiquated Policies

Winston Churchill continued to insist on military budget cuts for many years up until 1910. Britain had been at peace during the time that Lord Randolph was advocating these budget cuts. But when Churchill continued to advocate for such cuts, Britain was at war with the Boers. Germany was also steadily growing in military power and ambition.

In 1902, Arthur Balfour, Lord Salisbury's nephew, became Prime Minister. The Conservative Party took on a new policy which caused a lot of controversies. Free trade had been supported by both Liberal and Conservative Parties for 50 years, allowing trade with all nations on an equal basis. The Conservative Party had slowly begun moving towards a protectionist policy. This policy would grant a special financial concession to imports from the colonies. It was a policy they believed would help bind the Empire closer together. For there to be tariff relief, however, there needed to be tariffs in the first place. So, they proposed that there should be import duties on goods from countries not belonging to the Empire.

Churchill was certain his father would have supported free trade. Sir Francis Mowatt also urged Churchill to oppose the protectionism policy. This is exactly what he did, doggedly so.

Churchill attacked the policy and the Conservative Party

constantly. Already vulnerable on many points, such as the Anglo-Boer war, the Conservative Party began to view him as a traitor. This sentiment reached a climax in March 1904. As Churchill rose to speak, the Prime Minister left, followed shortly after by the entire Conservative Party jeering at Churchill as they filed out. Only the Liberals remained, who cheered him on.

Liberal Party

Winston Churchill realized at this point that he could no longer remain part of the Conservative Party. He approached the Liberal Party, and they were happy to give him a nomination. Churchill ran as the Liberal Party candidate for Northwest Manchester. On May 31, 1904, when Parliament resumed, Churchill took his seat on the Liberal side.

Churchill led the attack on Arthur Balfour. The tariff situation had divided the Conservative Party. Balfour, the Prime Minister and leader of the Conservatives, continued to sidestep the issue. In January 1906, a General Election took place. The Liberal Party won with a landslide majority. Arthur Balfour not only lost his government; he also lost his seat in Parliament.

Henry Campbell-Bannerman, a popular Liberal, became the new Prime Minister. Churchill was offered a Cabinet post. He chose the job of Under-Secretary of State for the Colonies. At the age of 31, Winston had reached Cabinet rank.

House of Lords

Winston Churchill and Lloyd George were central figures in British politics from 1908 to 1911, and they were good friends. Lloyd George had the position of Chancellor of the Exchequer. Churchill held a position in the Board of Trade. Together, George and Churchill devised a budget with tax proposals that targeted the rich. As anticipated, the reaction from the upper class was fierce.

It had been the tradition for the past 50 years that the House of Lords would not amend or reject any financial bill. The 1909 budget proposed by Lloyd George was passed by the House of Commons, but when it reached the House of Lords, they rejected it.

A general election was immediately called for by the Liberals. The Liberal Party returned to power. Churchill immediately set out to change the power held by the House of Lords. The Liberals announced their plan to reform the House of Lords. They would not be allowed to reject any money bills. The House of Lords could turn down other legislation, but it would still become the law if passed by the House of Commons in three successive sessions.

The Liberal Party called for another election to demonstrate the extent of their popular support. The results of the election were essentially the same as the previous one held that year. The bill was passed and went to the House of Lords. Pressure applied to the House of Lords ensured that they voted in favor of this new legislation. The power of the House of Lords to block legislation was destroyed in August 1911, when the new bill passed. Winston Churchill played a large part in the efforts of this new reform.

Home Secretary

Churchill then served as Home Secretary for several years. He focused primarily on prison reform. He also had to deal with several national strikes. Churchill used both police forces and the military in an attempt to maintain order and protect the British economy.

Churchill's actions in dealing with those strikes brought him the reputation of an enemy of the working class, a reputation that remained with him for the rest of his political career.

Chapter 6: World War I

The first hint of the clouds of war gathering occurred on July 1, 1911, with the Agadir crisis. A German gunboat appeared, uninvited, in the Moroccan port of Agadir. Morocco was a French protectorate at the time. The arrival of the German gunboat was to test international opinion.

French protests were expected. However, Germany expected the rest of Europe to remain silent and look the other way. What came as a shock was the reaction from Britain. As there were so many pacifists currently in power, Germany expected no response. Instead, Lloyd George spoke out. He delivered a stern warning, stating that Britain would not remain quiet and stand by idly when their country's interests were threatened.

The Germans withdrew their gunboat, and the Agadir crisis came to an end. The incident became a catalyst for Churchill's change in political outlook.

Britain's Might

For the first 11 years of his political career, Winston Churchill had focused on domestic issues. He took a pacifist stand for the most part. Once Lloyd George spoke out, Churchill practically changed his focus overnight. He became an advocate of British military strength in the struggle against aggression. Churchill saw the threat of Germany clearly for the first time, abandoning his policies of military budget cutbacks and pacifism.

The Prime Minister organized a Committee of Imperial Defence, and Churchill was invited to be a member. Winston went out of his way to learn what the state of Britain's military was.

The committee held its first meeting on August 23. The topic of discussion was what steps Britain would take if Germany attacked France.

It was quickly discovered during this discussion that the British Navy and the British Army had not had any joint planning sessions to discuss such an event. The British Navy felt they could handle any crisis on their own. They had made no provisions for cooperating with the British Army.

Lord Haldane, who headed up the War Office, proposed an expeditionary force. This force could cross the English Channel to back up the French forces. He had already made contact with French military planners who agreed.

In contrast, the Admiralty had made no plans for the possibility of transporting troops. In their view, the Army need not get involved at all. Where Lord Haldane had come presenting a strategic plan, the Navy had nothing to offer but faith in its capabilities.

Lord Haldane was furious and appealed to the Prime Minister, Herbert Henry Asquith, in a letter. He convinced the Prime Minister that the British Navy acting alone was not enough if Germany were to attack France. The Prime Minister also agreed that the head of the Admiralty would have to be replaced if he did not change his outlook.

Predictions

Churchill agreed with Lord Haldane's view. He prepared a memorandum titled "Military Aspects of the Continental Problem." The memorandum predicted that the French Army would not be able to stand against the German Army alone. He declared that by the 20th day, the French forces would be in full retreat. Churchill submitted his memorandum. General Henry Wilson, the Army spokesman, dismissed it completely. The memorandum was contrary to the official British position that the French Army could resist Germany alone.

First Lord of the Admiralty

Churchill and Lord Haldane continued to press the point of the Navy to the Prime Minister. The Prime Minister relented and gave the position of the First Lord of the Admiralty to Churchill.

The task of updating the Navy and making sure they were ready to fight a modern war fell to Winston Churchill at the age of 37.

Churchill took on the task with vigor. He set about establishing a Naval War Staff. Churchill also set about promoting younger officers, making him unpopular amongst some of the senior officers.

Churchill also asked retired Lord Fisher to return in a consulting capacity. Lord Fisher had served as First Sea Lord from 1904 to 1910.

In 1913 Churchill authorized a shift from coal to oil aboard all ships. He also authorized the installation of 15-inch guns. These guns had not been built or tested yet, but Churchill trusted the experts who said they would work. This gamble paid off and gave the British Navy an edge in the arms race.

Unrest at Home

All the new upgrades to the British Navy would require funding. In 1913 Churchill presented the highest naval budget in British history. The Cabinet was shocked. They requested the naval budget to be trimmed back. It was an interesting turn of events when you consider that Churchill had once advocated for the same. Surprisingly, it was Lloyd George who was now the most adamant that the naval budget be reduced.

George had continued to work on domestic reform in 1911 and 1912 while Churchill had been focusing all his energy and attention on the Navy. The once close comrades had drifted apart in their friendship. Now they openly clashed in Parliament. Lloyd George wanted more money for social reform. He went so far as to threaten to resign if the naval budget was not reduced.

Churchill did not back down. He responded by suggesting that he was considering rejoining the Conservative Party. Churchill also suggested that his resignation would bring the military operation to a standstill. The Prime Minister stepped in to calm both men down. A compromise was reached, where the Navy budget was slightly trimmed, and Lloyd George remained in the government.

The War Begins

The First World War began on June 28, 1914 with the assassination of Archduke Franz Ferdinand, heir to the throne of Austria. He was killed by a Slav nationalist while visiting Sarajevo. The Austro-Hungarian Empire demanded heavy reparations from Serbia for the assassination. Austria-Hungary declared war on Serbia after it refused to comply with the ultimatum. Serbia called on Russia's help. Russian forces were massed on the Austrian border. After Russia ignored the order to disperse their troops, Germany declared war on Russia.

Germany then invaded France without any formal declaration. They had marched through Belgium despite being denied permission. Germany made its declaration of war against France official on August 3. Britain officially entered the war on August 4, vowing to stand with their ally, France.

Churchill's work on preparing the British Navy paid off. In the first couple of months, the Navy did well. They managed to inflict losses on the enemy without suffering any of their own. The land forces were not doing as well. As Churchill had predicted in his memorandum, the French troops were retreating towards Paris by the third week. Their retreat left vital Channel ports in France exposed.

France requested Britain to send marines to Dunkirk and give the Germans an exaggerated idea of the British strength stationed along the coast. A diversion termed the Dunkirk Circus kicked into action.

Dunkirk Circus

Winston Churchill took part in the Dunkirk Circus enthusiastically. He supplied the marines with London buses covered in iron plating. These buses were not intended to fight. They were instead used to travel up and down the coast in well-advertised excursions. The timing of these excursions implied that the British were everywhere in the area. Churchill issued orders that the marines on the buses were to sing loudly and throw beer bottles into the streets to make sure that their presence could not go unnoticed. Churchill himself took part in the excursions.

Despite the comic nature, the Dunkirk Circus had the desired effect. Germany was deceived into believing there was a large British force and pulled back from the area.

Parliament, on the other hand, started growing annoyed because the First Lord of the Admiralty, Winston Churchill, was often absent. The Prime Minister frequently had to take charge of the Admiralty in Churchill's absence. Some members of Parliament even openly ridiculed Winston's actions. It was the beginning of Churchill's fall into disgrace.

Antwerp

The German Army's advance had been halted at the Battle of the Marne. The battle had taken a severe toll on French and Belgian forces. King Albert and the remainder of the Belgian troops were holding out at Antwerp. The Germans knew if they could take Antwerp, they would be able to continue to the Channel ports. If

Germany took the Channel ports, they would cut the Allies off.

The Germans began bombarding Antwerp on September 28. Four days later, King Albert sent an urgent request for reinforcements. It was clear that the fortifications of the city would not hold against the heavy German guns.

Lord Kitchener summoned Winston Churchill to his home in the late evening of October 2. He told Churchill that reinforcements could not be sent to Antwerp for another few days. Lord Kitchener asked Churchill to go to Antwerp at once in person and provide moral support. Churchill's task would be urging King Albert to hold out until the reinforcements reached Antwerp. Churchill left for Antwerp immediately.

After he arrived, Churchill took full control of the situation. As Lord Kitchener had hoped, his presence inspired the Belgians. At Churchill's request, Lord Kitchener dispatched two naval brigades to Antwerp. Churchill refused to return to Britain, remaining at Antwerp, leaving the Admiralty without its leader.

The naval brigades were not well-trained, but they fought valiantly under Churchill's direction. Despite all of Churchill's efforts, Antwerp fell five days after he arrived. The Conservative Party labeled Winston as an amateur Napoleon and blamed him for the loss of life.

In truth, the five days of delay Churchill managed to give the Allies held vital strategic value. It prevented the Germans from getting into a position where they could attack England. It also allowed the Belgian Army to escape safely.

Gallipoli Campaign

The British Navy began to suffer losses. Churchill's enemies began blaming his involvement in several activities, stating that he was neglecting his duty as the First Lord of the Admiralty.

Churchill began to turn his attention to Turkey. Turkey had entered the war on Germany's side in November. Consequently, the Czar of Russia had asked the Allies to help relieve the Turkish pressure on Russian troops in the Caucasus.

Lord Kitchener did not want to move his troops out of France. In a letter to Churchill, he stated that he did not think they could assist Russia in a meaningful way for several months. Citing that the only place they may have some effect on stopping reinforcements going east would be at the Dardanelles.

Churchill had an idea. Lord Kitchener was in control of the British Army, but Churchill had control of the British Navy. There was no real coordination between the two. Lord Kitchener was not going to commit soldiers to the Dardanelles. So, Churchill came up with a plan that involved a purely naval assault.

The plan involved naval bombardment on the outer fortresses of the straits. The British Navy would then sail through to Constantinople to defeat Turkey. This would allow them to set up a supply line from the Mediterranean countries to Russia.

Churchill presented his plan to the War Council. In a confusing session, it was somehow approved. The War Council was under the impression that "prepare" meant the Navy should get ready for an eventual expedition. Churchill took it as a go-ahead for immediate action.

Bombardment of the Turkish fortifications on the outer perimeter of the Dardanelles began on February 19, 1915. At first, the ships made good progress. Several fortresses fell, demoralizing the Turkish. Unfortunately, the fleet got bogged down, and their progress stalled.

Admiral de Robeck decided on a full-scale onslaught in March. Amassing all his ships, he opened fire on the inner forts. The first leg of his attack was very successful as he managed to put most of the fortresses out of commission. As the fleet moved forward, it encountered mines that had been missed by the advance force of minesweepers. Three battleships were sunk, and four more were damaged.

Admiral de Robeck immediately withdrew his ships pending additional minesweeping. He informed Churchill that he would not continue the attack for several days. Churchill urged him to continue, but the other admirals overruled him, refusing to interfere with the decision of the commander on the scene.

In later years, it was often written that had the attack continued, it may well have been successful and changed the course of World War I. The delay allowed the Turkish forces to replenish their ammunition and entrench themselves against any land forces that might arrive.

Lord Kitchener sent troops at Admiral de Robeck's request, but they only arrived in late April. They stormed the Gallipoli Peninsula at a cost of twenty thousand men and were barely able to keep the area.

German submarines had begun to enter the Mediterranean. With this new threat, the British ships began to withdraw. The operation was now a purely military one. After eight months at Gallipoli without progress, Allied troops were evacuated in December 1915.

Scapegoat

The Gallipoli Campaign resulted in a quarter of a million casualties with very little to show for it. There was a loud outcry, and people were demanding to know who was responsible for this blunder that cost so many lives.

The military blunder was quickly turning into a political one. Churchill insisted on keeping ships in the Dardanelles area. In frustration, Lord Fisher resigned. The public was turning against Churchill, as was evident from the many newspaper articles that attacked him.

The Conservative Party received a tip-off about Lord Fisher's resignation. They approached Lloyd George and informed him that unless Winston Churchill resigned, the Conservative Party would withdraw its support from the Liberal War Cabinet. The Conservative Party's withdrawal would threaten the Liberal Party's power.

The idea that there could be political feuding and a call for an election during a time of war was unthinkable. They agreed instead to form a coalition. Prime Minister Asquith concurred, as the alternative would bring his government down. Churchill received the news of the situation, as well as the demand for his resignation. He realized immediately that he was going to be used as the scapegoat for the failed Gallipoli campaign.

In the end, Churchill was demoted to Chancellor of the Duchy of Lancaster. This post was strictly ceremonial.

Churchill did not last long in his new role. He resigned on November 15, 1915, after only six months. A new War Committee had been formed, from which he was excluded, to replace the War Council. He no longer had a reason to remain in London.

Churchill decided that if he could no longer make a difference in the war on the political front, he would go to France in a military capacity.

Major Churchill

Winston Churchill requested a command position in the field. His request was granted, and Major Churchill left for France. He arrived at Boulogne on November 19, 1915. He immediately reported to the Commander-in-Chief of the British Expeditionary Force, Sir John French. French greeted Churchill courteously and asked how he wished to serve. Churchill replied that he was willing to take on any assignment.

French asked Churchill if he would take a brigade. Such a position meant that Churchill would be in command of four thousand men. Churchill was quick to accept but requested that he experience a month of trench warfare before taking the position.

Churchill joined the Grenadier Guards, front-line battalion, as a major. Initially, the battalion was not happy about his presence. They feared that an ex-Cabinet member would try to assert special privileges. Instead, Churchill spent the month on the front line, helping man the trenches and repairing barbed wire.

When the second-in-command took leave later that month, Churchill was asked to take over his duties, a clear sign that he had become popular amongst the Grenadier Guards. Churchill escaped death several times during this month, a fact that gave him the reputation of leading a charmed life.

After a month on the front line, Churchill returned to Sir John French's headquarters. He declared himself competent to take on the command of the promised brigade.

Unfortunately, while Churchill was on the front line, news of him preparing to take command of a brigade had reached Parliament. The Conservative Party was livid at the idea. The Prime Minister warned Sir John French that while Churchill may have the experience, he did not have the seniority, and the House of Commons would not tolerate Churchill taking command of a brigade. Churchill was instead made a lieutenant colonel and given the command of a battalion of the 6th Royal Scots Fusiliers.

The decision stung Churchill deeply and embittered him towards Prime Minister Asquith. However, Churchill mustered his enthusiasm and assumed command of his battalion. The battalion was stationed at Ploegsteert near Armentieres. It wasn't a remarkable unit, but Churchill was determined to transform them.

It took Churchill only a few days to win over his men. He charmed and entertained them as he shaped them into a first-rate unit. Churchill worked alongside them as they filled sandbags and strengthened trenches. His interest extended to every phase of the battalion's activity. He was also full of suggestions, even if some of them were not practical. News of Churchill's bravery filtered back to England. Articles were published in newspapers.

After four months in France, in March 1916 Churchill began to grow restless once more. He longed to return to Parliament, where he felt things were going awry. However, he knew he could not return so soon after his grand exit.

Churchill's opportunity to return to Parliament came in May. The 6th Royal Scots Fusiliers were amalgamated with another unit. Churchill was the junior of the two Commanding Officers involved and therefore had to surrender his command. Although he may well have been given a new battalion, Churchill decided to use the opportunity to return with honor to London. He asked to be relieved of his army commission with the understanding that he would not reapply.

Return to Parliament

In June 1916, Winston Churchill returned to Parliament. He returned as the Member for Dundee. For the first time in many years, Churchill held no special rank and was not a member of the active government.

Churchill felt as though he had been banished from the scene of action. He wrote a detailed report on the Gallipoli campaign in an attempt to vindicate himself. The Prime Minister refused to let him publish it because it could give information to the enemy.

Churchill struggled to accomplish anything in Parliament. He advocated the creation of a separate Air Ministry. This would lay the foundation for the creation of the Royal Air Force. He also attacked the strategy of Sir Douglas Haig, the current Commander-in-Chief. Sir Douglas Haig was currently waging the Battle of the Somme. His strategy was to beat the Germans in a war of attrition. Sir Douglas Haig believed that the Germans were losing men and materials at a higher rate than the Allies.

Churchill declared to the Cabinet in a memorandum that this was inaccurate. He stated the Allies were losing two or more men for each German soldier killed. It was an estimate that was later proven accurate.

Churchill went on to point out that the Allies had gained very little ground at Somme. Unfortunately, Churchill's memorandum went unheeded. Half a million British soldiers lost their lives in the Battle of the Somme, which dragged on for five months.

New Government

Prime Minister Asquith refused to allow Churchill to get a position in active office. For 20 months, Churchill was effectively in exile from office. He busied himself with painting. With furious dedication, typical of Churchill, he developed unquestionable talent.

Prime Minister Asquith's government was running into serious trouble. It was split from within and attacked from outside. The war was going badly. The Germans had overrun Rumania (now Romania) and Serbia. Bulgaria was now an enemy, and Russia was on the brink of revolution. At home, there were fresh troubles in Ireland.

An inquiry into the Dardanelles affair had at least exonerated Churchill to some degree. It cited that Prime Minister Asquith and Lord Kitchener also carried responsibility for what had taken place in their respective roles. There was a growing feeling that Prime Minister Asquith should step down. After a meeting outside Parliament, Bonar Law had agreed to Lloyd George's leadership. George presented Prime Minister Asquith with an ultimatum. Command of the war was to be taken from him and placed with an Inner Cabinet. As expected, Asquith refused, and George resigned. This move split the Liberal Party and destroyed Asquith's power. He had no choice but to resign as Prime Minister. George became the new Prime Minister with a coalition government.

Minister of Munitions

Lloyd George brought Churchill out of his exile, giving him the position of Minister of Munitions. Churchill immediately went about streamlining the administration, organizing effective channels of communication. Churchill would often personally visit the battle lines to ascertain what armaments and munitions were needed. He quickly mobilized Britain's resources and increased the strength of its Army noticeably.

Armistice Day

The final German offensive began in March 1918. The Germans were eager to attack before more American reinforcements arrived. They focused all their strength against France. The offensive lasted 40 days, but the British lines held. American troops began arriving by the hundred thousand, and the Germans were forced back.

Shortly after, World War I ended on November 11, 1918, the day of the Armistice. Churchill was presented with the Distinguished Service Medal for his accomplishments in producing arms for the American soldiers. He was the only Englishman to wear this decoration.

Chapter 7: Private Life

Winston Churchill was one of the most eligible bachelors amongst the British upper class for a long time. His standing dropped considerably when he left the Conservative Party to join the Liberal Party.

Winston shared a flat with his stockbroker brother, John. It was in the fashionable area of Mayfair in London. When he wasn't involved in Parliament, he played polo. He also played golf, but he was not very good at it.

Churchill was a frequent weekend guest at the homes of the upper class. He had ample opportunity to meet the most desired ladies. But it appeared as though Churchill was much too concerned with his career to allow himself to fall in love. A friend wrote of Churchill that he would often sit amongst them absorbed in his thoughts.

While campaigning in Dundee, Churchill met Clementine Hozier, a young, beautiful girl of 23. She not only had a lively spirit but was also very intelligent. Clementine also had a keen interest in politics. It was a perfect match.

The wedding took place at St. Margaret's Church, adjoining Westminster Abbey. The first leg of their honeymoon was spent at Blenheim Palace, the ancestral home of the Churchills. For the second leg, they spent time at Lake Maggiore in Italy. After the honeymoon, they returned to London to set up a modest home.

The marriage was very successful. Churchill would often consult his wife on a broad range of topics. There was never any rift between the pair, and they remained a loving couple.

They had five children in total. The eldest, Diana, was born in 1909. Randolph, their only son, was born in 1911. Sarah was born in 1914. Marigold was born in 1918 but sadly passed away as a child. Their last child was born in 1922, named Mary.

Churchill was so much a public figure that he is rarely thought of as a family man. But mindful of the treatment he received from his father, Churchill always made every attempt to establish meaningful relationships with his children. His son Randolph named his son Winston in his honor.

Diana married Duncan Sandys, a Minister in the Macmillan Cabinet. Mary married Christopher Soames, who also eventually held Cabinet positions. Unfortunately, not all his children's marriages were as successful as his own.

Sarah's first marriage ended in divorce, and her second husband, Anthony Beauchamp, committed suicide. Randolph's marriage also ended in divorce. He spent time in and out of Parliament, but his career there was unremarkable. Randolph was also involved in journalism.

Chapter 8: World War II

The day in 1939 that Britain declared war with Germany was the very same day that Winston Churchill assumed the post of First Lord of the Admiralty once more. Now acting at the voice of England, he threw himself into his task.

Churchill worked 18-hour days. He busied himself requisitioning new ships. He organized minesweeping operations and drew up plans for a blockade of the Baltic. Churchill also focused on hunting down German submarines. By the end of the year, Britain had sunk half of Germany's submarines. Churchill also served as the spokesman for the government.

Britain and many of the Allied countries held out hope that Germany would not advance further once they had taken Poland. They continued to hold out hope for peace. Churchill, on the other hand, continued to campaign against their complacency. He made several speeches against Hitler and tried to get neutral nations to enter the war against him.

Seven months after the war began, Germany invaded Denmark and Norway. Britain sent troops to support Norway, but it was an ill-prepared expedition that Churchill was against. British troops made no headway and were eventually evacuated.

Prime Minister Churchill

Parliament began calling for Prime Minister Chamberlain's resignation. They felt Chamberlain had not done enough to prepare for the war and that his leadership was too ambiguous. German forces then invaded Holland, Belgium, and Luxembourg.

After learning that he would not be fully supported in a coalition, Chamberlain called his Cabinet together and announced his resignation. Winston Churchill was the choice for the new Prime Minister. King George VI sent for Churchill that evening and asked him to name a Cabinet. Churchill was not specifically asked to form a coalition, but he decided that it was the only way to present a unified war effort. By the following morning, he had his first appointments ready. He named himself Minister of Defense in addition to his role as Prime Minister.

When Winston Churchill assumed the position of Prime Minister, it seemed as though Britain was alone in the war against Germany. Russia was allied with the enemy. A large portion of Europe had already fallen to Germany or was heavily overrun with German forces. France, Britain's old ally, was battered and struggling. Japan was beginning to threaten British Commonwealth territory in the Pacific. And America remained neutral.

Churchill, who had been in contact with American President Roosevelt, then sent his first communication to Roosevelt in his position as Prime Minister. He set about describing the current situation in Europe and followed this with a request. Churchill asked for a loan of older naval destroyers, several hundred aircraft, anti-aircraft guns, and ammunition. He concluded the communication by stating that he was looking to the Americans to keep the Japanese quiet.

President Roosevelt could not loan the destroyers without approval from Congress, and he felt it was not the right time to approach the subject. He did, however, promise Churchill he would do his best on the other materials required. President Roosevelt also made mention of the American fleet at Pearl Harbor in case of a war move from Japan.

Germany Advances

Germany continued steamrolling Europe. France had never really recovered from its losses in WWI and struggled to fight back. Eventually, their forces were bottled up in France.

Churchill obtained authorization from Parliament to exert practically unlimited and absolute power for the duration of the war. He immediately put into effect the regulation of every phase of British life. The purpose behind it was winning the war.

German forces reached the Atlantic Ocean, cutting the Allied forces into two. British forces were trapped in a narrowing pocket in Belgium. The German army continued to advance, and it was decided to evacuate British forces from Dunkirk.

Churchill was afraid that they would lose the bulk of their soldiers, as some 360,000 men were at Dunkirk. However, through a valiant effort using both naval and civilian vessels, 338,000 men made it out. The Royal Air Force played a huge role in this success, providing air cover from attacking German planes.

Winston Churchill delivered a speech on June 4, 1940. It was one of his most famous speeches.

"... we shall fight on the beaches, we shall fight on the fields and in the streets, we shall fight in the hills; we shall never surrender."

The end of this particular speech included words aimed specifically at America.

"In God's good time, the New World, with all its power and might, steps forth to the rescue and the liberation of the Old."

Churchill's words did not go unnoticed by President Roosevelt. Roosevelt realized that America would soon have to enter the war to preserve civilization. But he faced difficulties with domestic opinion.

The Battle of France

On June 5, Germany launched an offensive against France on a 70-mile (113-kilometer) front. By June 10, they had almost reached Paris. Italy then announced the end of its neutrality and declared war on the United Kingdom. France was falling rapidly. The French Premier, Paul Reynaud, evacuated from Paris with his government on June 12.

Churchill met with Reynaud at Briare and urged him to continue fighting and defending Paris. However, a defeatist attitude prevailed. Churchill returned to London knowing that the French would rather surrender than have their country laid to waste. On June 14, the Germans entered Paris. Philippe Petain took control of France on June 16 and entered into armistice negotiations with Germany. The German terms were accepted and came into effect on June 25. The Battle of France had come to an end.

Standing Alone

Britain stood alone against the Nazis, with Winston Churchill holding the nation together. Churchill anticipated that the Germans would soon attempt to cross the Channel and invade

Britain.

Germany had, in fact, initially planned to invade Britain but held back because of the inferiority of their Navy. They had switched their strategy into one of bombing and starving Britain into submission.

Churchill began preparing a counterattack. He focused his energy on amphibious warfare. Commando units were organized with the idea that they would lead in sudden strikes against the enemy.

Britain endured continuous bombing from German planes. Churchill held his country together with his oratory powers. He prevented them from cracking under German bombing pressure. Meanwhile, the British Army began to drive its way through Africa, pushing back the Italians. And the Royal Air Force continued to deal out heavy punishment across Europe.

Roosevelt was re-elected into the office of President of the USA. Once the election concluded, he was finally able to rally aid and sympathy for Britain. He transferred 50 American destroyers to Britain. In return, America got naval and air bases on various British possessions around the world.

The war continued, with Germany still gaining ground. In 1941, both Greece and Yugoslavia fell. It seemed as though Britain's days were numbered. Hitler regarded Britain as finished.

Germany Turns on Russia

In a move that has been hotly debated by historians, Hitler turned on Russia. Russia had been Germany's ally for two years, having signed a nonaggression treaty. On June 22, 1941, Hitler ignored the treaty and invaded Russia. He did so without a declaration of war; indeed, with no warning of any kind.

Churchill immediately offered an alliance with Stalin. Churchill's dislike of Communism was well known. It was a subject about which he had always been very vocal. In a speech, Churchill declared that any state who fought against Naziism would have Britain's aid. He continued to say that such matters of politics were currently unimportant in the light of what was unfolding.

The German army overextended itself in Russia. The retreating Russian army drew the German army ever deeper into its lands. When winter came, the German army found itself in trouble. They were far from home, ill-equipped to deal with the freezing weather, and unable to get supplies easily.

Atlantic Charter

Churchill and Roosevelt met in August 1941 to draft a declaration known as the Atlantic Charter. The meeting went well, and the

Charter was made public. In it was a declaration of mutual hatred for Nazi tyranny and a desire for world peace. America had come to realize the threat the Nazis posed on a global scale.

Roosevelt warned German ships to stay out of American waters. He also revised the Neutrality Act. This revision permitted armed U.S. ships to sail directly to British ports to deliver lend-lease materials. When the United States destroyer Kearney was torpedoed, notice was given to the American Navy to shoot on sight.

America Enters the War

On December 7, 1941, Japan attacked Pearl Harbor. At the same time, they began attacking the entire Malay Peninsula. Japanese attacks included the bombing of Hong Kong and Singapore, both British possessions at that time. Japan had, like Germany before it, given no warning and no declaration. Churchill reacted quickly, declaring war on Japan in reaction to the unprovoked attack.

With the attack on Pearl Harbor, America's view on the war changed instantly. The vote to join Britain in the declaration of war against Japan was almost unanimous. Germany, in return, declared war on America three days later.

Churchill, Roosevelt, and Stalin, nicknamed The Big Three, would often confer. Churchill often found himself acting as the mediator between Stalin and Roosevelt. He was the glue that held the alliance together. Even so, he remained wary of Stalin and Communism.

Churchill was concerned that Stalin would try to absorb as much of Eastern Europe as he could once Germany had been defeated. As before, his warnings went unheard.

D-Day

Churchill was actively involved in the planning of Operation Overlord. The Germans were expecting an attack, but they were uncertain as to when it would take place. Germany was convinced the invasion would strike across the Strait of Dover, landing at Calais. However, the actual target was Cherbourg and other points on the Normandy peninsula.

Churchill had planned to witness the event from a ship close to the coast, but King George convinced him not to go. Churchill's own Cabinet was against him being in the field as well.

D-Day took place on June 6, 1944. It was the biggest amphibious operation in history. Thousands of American and British soldiers fought their way ashore. Battleships and aircraft provided them with cover as they began their push to liberate France. D-Day marked the beginning of the final phase of WWII.

Yalta Conference

In February 1945 at Yalta, The Big Three met for the last time. France had been liberated, and the German thrust shattered at Bastogne. Only mop-up action remained in Europe. The purpose of the meeting was to work out the final plans for victory and establish the details of the postwar world. The issues of new borders and governments of the liberated states were also tackled at the Yalta Conference. A plan for the occupation of Germany was devised as well. Even the basis for the formation of the United Nations was discussed.

Victory

Russia eventually stormed Berlin and Hitler took his own life. Nazi Germany crumbled away. On Tuesday, May 8, 1945, the surrender officially came. Churchill announced the victory to a roaring ovation in the House of Commons. He then spoke to the British people from a balcony. The crowd sang jubilantly, as Churchill held up his fingers in his famous V for Victory sign.

Chapter 9: Post WWII

Churchill had hoped to continue the coalition government at least until the end of the war against Japan. He wished to continue as the head of the mixed government and help bring about the necessary social changes that would be required after the Nazis fell.

But the current government was already five years overdue for an election. With the pressures of war relieved, an election had to be held. The Labour Party made it clear it would not be part of the coalition after the war against Germany. Churchill was the leader of the Conservative Party. The election lines were being squared off already.

On May 23, 1945, Churchill presented his resignation. He was asked to form a caretaker government until elections could officially be held. The voting polls opened on July 5. The ballot boxes were sealed for three weeks, while they awaited the votes from the soldiers still abroad. The results were announced on July 26.

The Labour party won the majority. Churchill was forced to tender his resignation to the King, and Clement Attlee, the Labour Party leader, was asked to form a government.

Although he was 71 years old, Churchill refused to retire from public life. He remained in Parliament as the representative for the Woodford constituency. Churchill feared for the future of Britain, especially now with the socialist Labour Party in power. His fears did not materialize. Instead, the Labour Party carried out many needed reforms and brought Britain back to a position of economic strength.

Churchill was out of a significant position of power and not privy to meetings of the world leaders. He began to see the expansion of Communist world power. The world was slow to realize the danger that Stalin posed. So, Churchill began a crusade to awaken the West.

Iron Curtain

Westminster College in Fulton, Missouri, honored Churchill with a degree on March 5, 1946. He spoke at the ceremony. President Truman made the journey from Washington to introduce Churchill.

The war with Germany was only a few months past, and pro-Russian feeling was still high in both Britain and America. In Eastern Europe, Stalin had already begun his campaign. Yet people still clung to the hope of Stalin's peaceful intentions.

Churchill opened people's eyes in his magnificent speech delivered at Westminster College. He called for an alliance between America and Britain. Churchill also used the phrase "iron curtain" as he warned them about Soviet Russia.

As with many of Churchill's predictions, he was correct about the dangers of the Soviet Union. But not unlike many of Churchill's predictions, his warning went unheeded. The speech was described as shocking and, overall, was badly received. By 1948 the Soviets had extended their control over East Germany, Hungary, Albania, Romania, Poland, and Czechoslovakia.

Prime Minister Once More

Churchill became the Prime Minister once again in the 1951 election. His prime concern during this time of his administration was preserving world peace. He attempted to arrange a friendly meeting between Eisenhower, Malenkov (the short-lived successor to Stalin), and himself. Churchill believed that better communication between the East and the West would help ease tensions. Unfortunately, such a meeting would not take place until after Churchill was no longer in power.

Queen Elizabeth II bestowed the Order of the Garter on Churchill in 1953 and with this came the title of knighthood. Later that year

Churchill was awarded the Nobel Prize for Literature in recognition of his many exceptional works.

Prime Minister Churchill's eightieth birthday in November 1954 was a grand affair. Churchill's Cabinet members urged him to retire in light of an upcoming election. And so, on April 5, 1955, he announced his resignation. Churchill did, however, retain his seat in Parliament.

In his retirement, Churchill kept himself busy. He traveled, painted, and continued his writing work.

Passing of Greatness

On January 12, 1965, Churchill suffered a devastating stroke. He had suffered strokes before, but this would prove to be his last. On January 24, 1965, Winston Churchill passed away. He was given a state funeral on January 30; an honor usually reserved only for royals.

Many memorials have been dedicated to Winston Churchill. His statue was unveiled in Parliament Square in 1973. He was granted honorary citizenship of the United States; one of only eight people to receive this. In 1999 the U.S. Navy named one of their destroyers the USS Winston S. Churchill.

Chapter 10: Legacy

More than 50 years after his passing, Winston Churchill remains an important figure. He excelled as a public servant and was an orator of rare power. But his talents did not stop there. He was a historian, a biographer, a painter, and a soldier of courage and distinction.

Speeches

The speeches he delivered had a massive impact on the world, and he is still often quoted. Churchill would write out his speeches in advance, putting much thought into the words. He would commit his speeches to memory before delivering them with strength and vigor. What many are unaware of is that Churchill had a slight lisp.

His most well-known and famous speeches were delivered during World War II. The first of these is known as "Blood, Toil, Tears, and Sweat," delivered on May 13, 1940. The speech known as "We Shall Fight on the Beaches" was delivered on June 4, 1940. Churchill also delivered a speech in the House of Commons on June 18, 1940, known as "This was Their Finest Hour." The speech was also broadcast over the BBC.

Writing

Winston Churchill wrote several books during his lifetime. Below is a list of the books Churchill authored:

- *The Story of the Malakand Field Force* (1898)
- *The River War* (1899)
- *Savrola* (1899)
- *London to Ladysmith via Pretoria* (1900)
- *Ian Hamilton's March* (1900)
- *Mr. Brodrick's Army* (1903)
- *Lord Randolph Churchill* (1906)
- *For Free Trade* (1906)
- *My African Journey* (1908)
- *Liberalism and the Social Problem* (1909)
- *The People's Right* (1910)
- *The World Crisis* (1923-31)
- *My Early Life: A Roving Commission* (1930)
- *India* (1931)
- *Thoughts and Adventures / Amid These Storms* (1932)
- *Marlborough: His Life and Times* (1933-38)
- *Great Contemporaries* (1937)
- *Arms and the Covenant / While England Slept* (1938)
- *Step by Step 1936-1939* (1939)
- *Into Battle / Blood Sweat and Tears* (1941)
- *The Unrelenting Struggle* (1942)

- *The End of the Beginning* (1943)
- *Onwards to Victory* (1944)
- *The Dawn of Liberation* (1945)
- *Victory* (1946)
- *War Speeches* (1940-1945)
- *Secret Session Speeches* (1946)
- *The Second World War* (1948-53)
- *The Sinews of Peace* (1948)
- *Painting as a Pastime* (1948)
- *Europe Unite* (1950)
- *In the Balance* (1951)
- *The War Speeches Definitive Edition* (1951-53)
- *Stemming the Tide* (1953)
- *A History of the English-Speaking Peoples* (1956-58)
- *The Unwritten Alliance* (1961)

Churchill also wrote many essays during his life on a variety of topics.

Controversy

In light of today's society, some of the things that Winston Churchill said and did would be, and are seen as, extremely controversial. They are often debated and used in a negative way against him.

Granting women the right to vote, for example, was something that he found rather silly. Some experts call him racist, saying that he deemed the British people superior to the indigenous people of the areas Britain colonized. Others say it would be unfair to judge him by the more modern attitudes and beliefs we hold today, especially considering that those beliefs were widely held during that period of history.

Other points of controversy include Churchill's firm belief in imperialism. He always held a romanticized view of both the British Empire and the reigning monarch. It was because of this view that Churchill was against self-rule for India. He also viewed Mahatma Gandhi as a threat to the British Empire.

When Gandhi launched his Quit India Movement in 1942, Churchill convinced himself that Gandhi was acting on behalf of the Axis powers. Churchill was also convinced that Gandhi was taking a glucose supplement during his famed prison fast. It was only once the Labour Party was in power that formal negotiations for a transfer of power back to India began.

Relevance Today

Although a historical figure, Winston Churchill remains relevant today. Many of the reforms he enacted in his time as a politician laid the foundations of the regulations currently used in the United Kingdom.

It is also easy to argue that the World Wars, especially WWII, could have had a dramatically different outcome if it was not for the influence of Churchill. But Churchill's relevance extends beyond these points.

Technological advancement was something Churchill often pondered. Even in 1939, he was concerned that the newspapers were influencing people as he wrote, "The newspapers do a lot of thinking for us." If you were to substitute the word newspapers for media, the relevance of this statement still holds true today. Churchill felt that such a process would produce "standardized citizens, all equipped with regulation opinions, prejudices, and sentiments, according to their class or party."

It's a chilling thought indeed when you take into account what is happening in the world today.

In an essay Churchill wrote in 1924, titled "Shall We All Commit Suicide?" he forecast the dangers of technological development on the military front. And in his essay "Fifty Years Hence," he laid bare his thoughts on technological developments. He was concerned that while the modern age may bring many modern wonders, the nature of human beings remains largely unchanged, and under sufficient stress, humans are capable of committing terrible deeds.

Courage and Endurance

Churchill's value lies not only in all that he accomplished within his lifetime. It lies with Churchill's approach and the broad principles that motivated him. It lies with the leadership he showed, especially in times of crisis. It lies with the foresight he showed and the personality that he was. And most importantly it lies with the courage and endurance that Churchill displayed throughout his lifetime.

"What is the use of living, if it not be to strive for noble causes and to make this muddled world a better place for those who will live in it after we are gone?" - Sir Winston Churchill

Conclusion

Winston Churchill was a man who confidently believed in having a great destiny. He would throw himself completely into whatever task or job he undertook without fear. Unafraid to lead with innovation, he was often called a Renaissance man in later years.

Though often embroiled in controversy, Churchill valued his own ideals above whatever political party he happened to be with. He was often perceived as motivated by personal ambition. Despite this, Churchill genuinely loved his country and its people. He was a straightforward man who did not involve himself in political intrigue.

Throughout his life, Churchill correctly predicted the outcome of many situations. But he seemed to be cursed, as nobody paid heed to his warnings. Churchill always displayed astonishing insight and foresight—not only in military matters, but in the movement of world powers as well.

In the area of technology, Churchill was unafraid. He championed the development of the tank, and he was quick to realize the value of aircraft. A man who participated in one of the last great cavalry charges, Churchill lived to discuss the problems of warfare in the atomic age.

Although excited by war, he was not indifferent to the suffering it caused. He was often on the side of being gentle toward the defeated enemy, despite the controversy this often caused.

For 60 years, Winston Churchill lived in the public eye. Many times, he was a figure of public scorn and anger. And at other times, he was a figure of heroism and unmatched grandeur. Whatever people felt towards him, nobody can deny that he was one of the greatest figures of his time. The influence of Winston Churchill will be felt long into the future.

www.ingramcontent.com/pod-product-compliance
Lightning Source LLC
LaVergne TN
LVHW011737060526
838200LV00051B/3217